THE POWER OF
ATTITUDE

by
John C. Maxwell

RIVER
OAK
PUBLISHING

All scripture quotations are taken from the *King James Version* of the Bible.

All quotations without attribution are assumed to be anonymous.

The Power of Attitude
ISBN 1-58919-397-0
Copyright © 2001 by John C. Maxwell

Published by RiverOak Publishing
P.O. Box 700143
Tulsa, Oklahoma 74170-0143

Introduction

Attitude ...

It is the reflection of our true selves.
Its roots are inward, but its fruit is outward.
It is our best friend—or our worst enemy.
It is more honest and more consistent than our words.
It is a future outlook based on past experiences.
It draws people to us—or repels them.
It is never content until it is expressed.
It is the librarian of our past.
It is the speaker of our present.
It is the prophet of our future.

The quotes and insights in this book have been gleaned from a lifetime of positive thinking and learning. I found out a long time ago that maintaining a positive attitude is the key to personal success in life. Read, learn, and file these ideas. Then go out and live them, with power!

—John C. Maxwell

I have often thought that the best way
to define a man's character would be
to seek out the particular mental or
moral attitude in which, when it came
upon him, he felt himself most deeply
and intensely active and alive.

—William James

_____

As he thinketh in his heart, so is he.

—Proverbs 23:7

Your are only an attitude
away from success!

—John C. Maxwell

The highest reward for man's toil
is not what he gets for it but
what he becomes by it.

—John Ruskin

———————————————

It's not whether you get knocked
down, it's whether you get up.

—Vince Lombardi

All our dreams can come true—
if we have the courage to pursue them.

—Walt Disney

In the middle of difficulty
lies opportunity.

—Albert Einstein

_____

The successful man will profit
from his mistakes and try again
in a different way.

—Dale Carnegie

What lies behind us and what
lies before us are tiny matters
compared to what lies within us.

— Walt Emerson

I may not be able to change the world
I see around me, but I can change
the way I see the world within me.

———————————————

Your attitude determines
your action. Your action
determines your accomplishment.

—John C. Maxwell

We cannot direct the wind ...

but we can adjust the sails.

If you think you are beaten, you are.
If you think you dare not, you don't.
If you'd like to win but think you can't,
It's almost certain you won't.

_____

Life's battles don't always go
To the stronger or faster man,
But sooner or later, the man who wins
Is the man who thinks he can.

A successful man is one who can
lay a firm foundation with the bricks
others have thrown at him.

—David Brinkley

If things go wrong, don't go with them.

—Roger Babson

You are today where your
thoughts have brought you;
you will be tomorrow where
your thoughts take you.

—James Allen

Winning is not everything—
but making the effort to win is.

—Vince Lombardi

You never achieve real success
unless you like what you are doing.

—Dale Carnegie

You and I do not see things as they are.
We see things as we are.

—Herb Cohen

Whether you think you can or
think you can't—you are right.

—Henry Ford

17

I have learned that success is to be
measured not so much by the position
that one has reached in life as by the
obstacles which one has overcome
while trying to succeed.

—Booker T. Washington

_____

Our attitude toward things is likely
to be more important than
the things themselves.

—A.W. Tozer

Happiness depends not upon things
around me, but on my attitude.
Everything in my life will
depend on my attitude.

—Alfred A. Montapert

The quickest way to correct the other
fellow's attitude is to correct your own.

—King Vidor

_____

It's your attitude, not your aptitude,
that will determine your altitude.

God chooses what we go through;
we choose how we go through it.

—John C. Maxwell

It is a fact that you project
what you are.

—Norman Vincent Peale

Life is not a dress rehearsal.

—John C. Maxwell

A pessimist is a person who,
regardless of the present, is
disappointed in the future.

Do not let what you cannot do
interfere with what you can do.

—John Wooden

We cannot continually behave
in a manner that is inconsistent
with the way we see ourselves.

Quitting is a permanent solution
to a temporary problem.

The greatest discovery of our
generation is that human beings
can alter their lives by altering
their state of mind.

—William James

There is no wrong side of the bed.
We get up on the wrong side
of our mind.

The greatest mistake a person
can make is doing nothing.

—John C. Maxwell

It is the eye that makes the horizon.

—Ralph Waldo Emerson

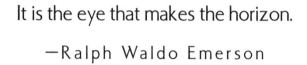

Believe you are defeated,
believe it long enough, and
it is likely to become a fact.

—Norman Vincent Peale

What really matters is what
happens in us, not to us.

Every man takes the limits of
his own field of vision for
the limits of the world.

—Arthur Schopenhauer

_____

As he thinketh in his heart, so is he.

—Proverbs 23:7

Men may be measured by
their reactions to life's inequities.

The environment you fashion out of …
your thoughts … your beliefs …
your ideals … your philosophy … is
the only climate you will ever live in.

—Alfred A. Montapert

Health, happiness, and prosperity
are primarily mental.

—Marian Ramsay

Life is formed from the inside out.
What I am inside determines
the issues in the battle of life.

—Dr. William Hornaday

Very little is needed to make
a happy life. It is all within yourself—
in your way of thinking and attitude.

—Fred Corbett

_____

Man's greatness lies in
his power of thought.

—Blaise Pascal

Others can stop you temporarily,
but you're the only one
who can do it permanently.

—John C. Maxwell

An optimist may see a light where
there is none, but why must the
pessimist always run to blow it out?

—Michel de Saint-Pierre

Growl all day and you'll
feel dog tired at night.

Man must cease attributing
his problems to his environment
and learn again to exercise his will.

—Albert Schweitzer

We lost because we
told ourselves we lost.

—Leo Tolstoy

Be careful for nothing, prayerful
for everything, thankful for anything.

—Dwight L. Moody

Never look back unless
you want to go that way.

If a man has Limburger cheese
on his upper lip, he thinks
the whole world smells.

—John C. Maxwell

_____

I go at what I do as if there
were nothing else in
the world for me to do.

—Charles Kingsley

Places and circumstances
never guarantee happiness.
You must decide within yourself
whether you want to be happy.

—Robert J. Hastings

Failure is only the opportunity
to begin again more intelligently.

—Henry Ford

_____

Opportunity looks bigger
going than coming.

Action and feeling go together,
and by regulating the action, . . .
we can directly regulate the feeling.

—William James

The quality of a person's life is in
direct proportion to their commitment
to excellence, regardless of their
chosen field of endeavor.

—Vince Lombardi

Whatever you do, work at it
with all your heart, as working
for the Lord, not for men.

—Colossians 3:23 NIV

Always bear in mind that our
own resolution to succeed is more
important than any other one thing.

—Abraham Lincoln

To live a long time and to enjoy life,
the unseen force for you to
develop is the proper attitude.

—Alfred A. Montapert

The quality of an individual is
reflected in the standards
they set for themselves.

—Ray Kroc

The purpose of human life is
to serve, and to show compassion
and the will to help others.

—Albert Schweitzer

The man who acquires the ability to
take full possession of his own mind
may take possession of anything
else to which he is justly entitled.

—Andrew Carnegie

Who is rich? He that
rejoices in his portion.

—Benjamin Franklin

48

Nothing is as hard as it looks;
everything is more rewarding
than you expect; and if anything
can go right it will and at the
best possible moment.

—Maxwell's Law

I thank God for my handicaps,
for through them I have found
myself, my work, and my God.

—Helen Keller

Where there is no hope in the future,
there is no power in the present.

—John C. Maxwell

There is no security in this life,
only opportunity.

—General Douglas MacArthur

Success is peace of mind in
knowing you did your best.

—John Wooden

_____

Anyone who stops learning is old,
whether at twenty or eighty.
Anyone who keeps
learning stays young.

—Henry Ford

Football games are generally won
by the boys with the greatest desire.

—Paul "Bear" Bryant

The attitude of the individual
determines the attitude of the group.

—John C. Maxwell

———————————

If a man has done his best,
what else is there?

—General George S. Patton

The last of the human freedoms
is to choose one's attitude in
any given set of circumstances.

—Victor Frankl,
survivor of Nazi concentration camp

It is no exaggeration to say
that a strong, positive self-image
is the best possible preparation
for success in life.

—Dr. Joyce Brothers

_____

Misery is an option!

I expect the best and with
God's help will attain the best.

—Norman Vincent Peale

You never get ahead of
anyone as long as you try
to get even with them.

_____

Maintaining the right attitude is
easier than regaining the right attitude.

I firmly believe that any man's finest
hour—his greatest fulfillment to
all he holds dear—is that moment
when he has worked his heart out in
a good cause and lies exhausted
on the field of battle—victorious.

—Vince Lombardi

Don't let yourself ...

WORRY when you're doing your best.

HURRY when success depends on accuracy.

THINK evil of anyone
until you have the facts.

BELIEVE a thing is
impossible without trying it.

Aim for the highest.

—Andrew Carnegie

Even a mistake may turn out
to be the one thing necessary
to a worthwhile achievement.

—Henry Ford

THE POWER OF
ATTITUDE

Nothing can stop the man with the
right mental attitude from achieving
his goal; nothing on earth can help the
man with the wrong mental attitude.

—W.W. Ziege

I'm not sure all happy people are
generous, but I've never seen a
generous person who wasn't happy.

Life is like baseball;
it's 95% mental and
the other half is physical.

—Yogi Berra

If you want to change attitudes,
start with a change in behavior.
In other words, begin to act the part,
as well as you can, of the person you
would rather be, the person you most
want to become. Gradually, the old,
fearful person will fade away.

—Dr. William Glasser

Attitudes determine actions.
You are not what you think you are.
What you think, you are!

Accept the challenges so that you
may feel the exhilaration of victory.

—General George S. Patton

People catch our spirit just
like they catch our colds—
by getting close to us.

Every man over forty is responsible
for [the disposition of] his face.

—Abraham Lincoln

A happy person is not a person
in a certain set of circumstances,
but rather a person with
a certain set of attitudes.

—Hugh Downs

———————————

Instead of saying TGIF, say TGIT—
Thank God it's today!

Keep your face to the sunshine and
you cannot see the shadows.

—Helen Keller

Afflictions color your life,
but you choose the color.

_____

People don't care how much
you know until they know
how much you care.

—John C. Maxwell

Sales are not made or unmade
inside the prospect's office.
They are made or unmade inside you.

—Brian Azar

Wars may be fought with weapons, but they are won by men. It is the spirit of the men who follow and of the man who leads that gains victory.

—General George S. Patton

It is unfortunate when people allow themselves to get like concrete— all mixed up and permanently set.

Well done is better than well said.

—Benjamin Franklin

Your attitude is the outward
expression of an inward feeling.

—John C. Maxwell

Dread disease is the
hardening of the attitude.

Success or failure in business is
caused more by the mental attitude
than by mental capacities.

Man creates his environment—
mental, emotional, and physical—
by the attitude he develops.

Life is either a daring
adventure or nothing.

—Helen Keller

We are either the masters
or the victims of our attitudes.
It is a matter of personal choice—
blessing or curse.

Every change in human attitude
must come through internal
understanding and acceptance.
Man is the only known creature
who can reshape and remold
himself by altering his attitude.

—John C. Maxwell

Always do more than
is required of you.

—General George S. Patton

Don't find fault. Find a remedy.

—Henry Ford

A positive mental attitude is
rooted in clear, calm, and
honest self-confidence.

Every problem has in it the seeds
of its own solution. If you don't have
any problems, you don't get any seeds.

—Norman Vincent Peale

You are where you are and what you
are because of the dominating
thoughts that occupy your mind.

—John C. Maxwell

_____

Do you see the green near
every sand trap, or the sand traps
around every green?

The situation you live in
doesn't have to live in you.

—Roberta Flack

THE POWER OF
ATTITUDE

The good news is that the bad news
can be turned into good news
when you change your attitude.

—Robert Schuller

Our children are like mirrors—
they reflect our attitudes in life.

Attitude is the criterion for success.
But you can't buy an attitude
for a million dollars.
Attitudes are not for sale.

—Denis Waitley

The higher you go in
any organization of value,
the better the attitude you'll find.

—John C. Maxwell

Man who say it cannot be done
should not interrupt man doing it.

—Chinese Proverb

Beware of those who stand aloof
and greet each venture with reproof;
the world would stop if things were run
by men who say, "It can't be done."

There is no sadder sight
than a young pessimist.

—Mark Twain

We are confronted with
insurmountable opportunities.

—Walt Kelley

Never accept the negative
until you have thoroughly
explored the positive.

A person cannot travel
within and stand still without.

—James Allen

———————————

Nothing will be attempted
if all possible obstacles
must first be removed.

—Samuel Johnson

My great concern is not whether
you have failed, but whether you
are content with your failures.

−Abraham Lincoln

THE POWER OF
ATTITUDE

When you affirm big, believe big,
and pray big, big things happen.

—Norman Vincent Peale

We cannot tailor make the situations
of our life, but we can tailor make the
attitudes to fit them before they arrive.

Failure isn't failure unless
you don't learn from it.

—Dr. Ronald Niednagel

Every success I know has been
reached because the person was able
to analyze defeat and actually profit
from it in the next undertaking.

—William Marston

Laughter is the shortest distance
between two people.

—Victor Borge

If you have a will to win,
you have achieved half your success;
if you don't, you have achieved
half your failure.

—David Ambrose

Life is 10 percent how we make it;
90 percent how we take it.

Circumstances do not make you
what you are ... they reveal
what you are!

—John C. Maxwell

You can get everything in life
you want if you help enough other
people get what they want.

—Zig Ziglar

Of all the things you wear, your
expression is the most important.

_____

If a man be gracious and courteous
to strangers, it shows he
is a citizen of the world.

Ninety-nine percent of failures
come from people who have
the habit of making excuses.

—George Washington Carver

It is what you learn after
you know it all that counts.

—John Wooden

Lord, grant that I may always desire
more than I can accomplish.

—Michelangelo

Again and again, the impossible
problem is solved when we see
that the problem is only a tough
decision waiting to be made.

—Robert Schuller

You're more likely to act
yourself into feeling, than
feel yourself into action.

—Jerome Bruner

Many intelligent people never
move beyond the boundaries
of their self-imposed limitations.

—John C. Maxwell

Always help people increase
their own self-esteem.
Develop your skill in making
other people feel important.

—Donald Laird

Events are less important
than our responses to them.

—John Hersey

_____

When opportunity knocks, a grumbler
complains about the notice.

I got a simple rule about everybody.
If you don't treat me right—
shame on you!

—Louis Armstrong

Any manager who can't get along
with a .400 hitter is crazy.

—Joe McCarthy,
New York Yankees

Always make others feel needed,
important, and appreciated and
they'll return the same to you.

—John C. Maxwell

An optimist is a driver who thinks
that empty space at the curb
won't have a hydrant beside it.

— Changing Times

Optimism is the cheerful frame of
mind that enables a teakettle to sing,
though in hot water up to its nose.

_____

A pessimist is one who makes
difficulties of his opportunities;
an optimist is one who makes
opportunities of his difficulties.

—Reginald B. Mansell

When one door closes, another opens;
but we often look so long and so
regretfully upon the closed door
that we do not see the one
which has opened for us.

—Alexander Graham Bell

Think right, act right; it is
what you think and do that
makes you what you are.

———————————

Your attitude speaks so loudly
that I can't hear what you say.

Some people look at things as they
are and say, "Why?" I look at things
as they can be and say, "Why not?"

—Robert Kennedy

Your problem is not your problem.
Your attitude—how you handle
your problem—is your problem.

—John C. Maxwell

The greatest mistake one can
make in life is to be continually
fearing you will make one.

—Elbert Hubbard

Unless you try to do something
beyond what you have already
mastered, you will never grow.

—Ronald E. Osborn

You have not lived today until you
have done something for someone
who can never repay you.

—John Bunyan

We all have possibilities we don't
know about. We can do things
we don't even dream we can do.

—Dale Carnegie

Each day we need good thoughts
to live by. And remember ...
you get what you order in life.

—Alfred A. Montapert

Instead of giving people
a piece of your mind, give them
a piece of your positive attitude.

———————————

To the discontented man
no chair is easy.

—Benjamin Franklin

A difficult crisis can be more readily
endured if we retain the conviction
that our existence holds a purpose—
a cause to pursue, a person
to love, a goal to achieve.

—John C. Maxwell

If you can't fight and
you can't flee ... flow.

—Robert Eliot

Worry does not help anything,
but it hurts everything.

—General George S. Patton

Become a possibilitarian. No matter
how dark things seem to be or
actually are, raise your sights and
see possibilities—always see them,
for they're always there.

—Norman Vincent Peale

Our attitude at the beginning of
a task will affect its outcome
more than anything else.

—John C. Maxwell

_____

Unless a man undertakes more
than he possibly can do,
he will never do all he can do.

—Henry Drummond

Coaches who can outline plays
on a blackboard are a dime a dozen.
The ones who win get inside
their players and motivate.

It doesn't pay to worry. If you went
through last year's files marked
"important," chances are the only
things you'd keep are the paper clips.

—Robert Orben

_____

Success is going from failure to
failure without loss of enthusiasm.

—Abraham Lincoln

My attitude has always been …
if it's worth playing, it's worth
paying the price to win.

—Paul "Bear" Bryant

The person interested in success
has to learn to view failure as
a healthy, inevitable part of the
process of getting to the top.

—Dr. Joyce Brothers

We tend to get what we expect.

—Norman Vincent Peale

The human spirit is never finished
when it is defeated ... it is finished
when it surrenders.

—Ben Stein

The man who goes farthest is generally the one who is willing to do and dare. The "sure-thing" boat never gets far from the shore.

—Dale Carnegie

Most people are very close to becoming the person God wants them to be.

—John C. Maxwell

Leadership has less to do with position
than it does with disposition.

Psychosclerosis: the hardening
of the attitude which causes
a person to cease dreaming,
seeing, thinking, and leading.

—Ashley Montague

We cannot hold a torch
to light another's path
without brightening our own.

—Ben Sweetland

Before a person can achieve
the kind of life he wants, he must
think, act, walk, talk, and conduct
himself in all of his affairs as would
the person he wishes to become.

—Zig Ziglar

Those folks who succeed simply
remain enthusiastic longer
than those who fail.

—Ralph Waldo Emerson

We make a living by what we get, but
we make a life by what we give.

—Winston Churchill

Winners concentrate on winning;
losers concentrate on getting by.

—John C. Maxwell

Any fact facing us is not as important
as our attitude toward it, for that
determines our success or failure.

—Norman Vincent Peale

People who never do any more
than they get paid for, never get
paid for any more than they do.

An optimist sees an
opportunity in every calamity;
a pessimist sees a calamity
in every opportunity.

—Herbert V. Prochnow

It is your actions and attitude
when you are on your own
that reflect what you really are.

—Martin Vanbee

_____

Attitudes are nothing more
than habits of thought ...
and habits can be acquired.

—Paul J. Meyer

Our attitude toward life determines
life's attitude toward us.

—John C. Maxwell

Your attitude tells the world
what you can expect from life.

_____

Nothing can stop the person
with the right attitude from
pursuing his goal.

Ability is what you're
capable of doing. Motivation
determines what you do.
Attitude determines
how well you do it.

—Lou Holtz

Ninety percent of all those who
fail are not actually defeated ...
they simply quit.

—Paul J. Meyer

Start a crusade in your life
to be your very best.

—William Danforth

Enthusiasm and persistence can
make an average person superior;
indifference and lethargy can
make a superior person average.

—William Ward

It's not where you start—
it's where you finish that counts.

—Zig Ziglar

_____

All looks yellow to the jaundiced eye.

—Alexander Pope

There is little difference in people,
but that little difference makes a
big difference. The little difference
is attitude. The big difference is
whether it is positive or negative.

—Clement Stone

Gratitude is the least of virtues; but
ingratitude the worst of vices.

———————————

Two men looked through prison bars—
one saw mud, the other stars.

[It is] tragic when we put off living.
We dream of a magical rose garden
over the horizon and miss the roses
blooming outside our windows.

—Dale Carnegie

Do a little more each day than
you think you possibly can.

—Lowell Thomas

_____

Superiority—doing things
a little better than anybody
else can do them.

—Orison Swett Marden

Chance favors the prepared mind.

—Louis Pasteur

True greatness consists in
being great in little things.

—Charles Simmons

We are what we repeatedly do.
Excellence, then, is not
an act but a habit.

Since your thinking has
a direct bearing on your
performance, your thinking
must be based on sound input.

—Zig Ziglar

Commitment:
another name for success.

_____

The only alternative
to perseverance is failure.

I don't know what your destiny
will be, but one thing I know:
The only ones among you who will be
really happy are those who will have
sought and found how to serve.

—Albert Schweitzer

There is always a best way
of doing everything.

—Ralph Waldo Emerson

Nothing would be done at all
if a man waited until he could do it so
well that no one could find fault with it.

—Cardinal Newman

If thinking is viewed as a skill …
it can be improved by practice,
as we improve other skills.

THE POWER OF
ATTITUDE

I started where the last man left off.

—Thomas Edison

_____

I can do small things in a great way.

—James Freeman Clarke

Anybody who accepts mediocrity—
in school, on the job, in life—
is a person who compromises,
and when the leader compromises,
the whole organization compromises.

—Charles Knight

Behind every great idea is
someone saying, "It won't work."

_____

Great things are not done
by impulse but by a series of
small things brought together.

There is no speed limit in
the pursuit of excellence.

Progress is not created
by contented people.

—Frank Tyger

———————————

I do the very best I know how—
the very best I can; and I mean to
keep on doing so until the end.

—Abraham Lincoln

The greatest reward for doing
is the opportunity to do more.

—Jonas Salk

About the Author

John Maxwell is one of the world's most respected authorities on leadership and personal effectiveness. He has written more than twenty books, including the *New York Times* best seller *The 21 Irrefutable Laws of Leadership,* which has sold more than half a million copies. In addition to his writing career, he is a popular speaker, inspiring more than 250,000 people annually at appearances nationwide.

Dr. Maxwell's advice is based on his thirty-plus years of experience as a pastoral and organizational leader. He is founder of the INJOY Group, an organization that helps people maximize their personal and leadership potential. And he has served as a senior pastor for churches in California, Ohio, and Indiana.

The father of two grown children, Dr. Maxwell lives in Atlanta, Georgia, with Margaret, his wife of more than twenty-five years.

Additional copies of this book and other titles by John C. Maxwell
are available from your local bookstore.

The Power of Leadership
The Power of Influence
The Power of Thinking Big

RIVER
OAK
PUBLISHING